The BUILD Framework®

The BUILD Framework®

*A Heart-Based System for Personal
and Professional Growth*

John Peitzman

www.buildheart.com

The BUILD Framework®: A Heart-Based System for Personal and Professional Growth

Published by Build Heart Publishing

Copyright © 2019 by John Peitzman

Build Heart Publishing
655A Darling Street
Rozelle, NSW 2039
Email: publishing@buildheart.com

Limit of Liability/Disclaimer of Warranty:

Publishing and editorial team:
Author Bridge Media, www.AuthorBridgeMedia.com
Project Manager and Editorial Director: Helen Chang
Editor: Jenny Shipley
Publishing Manager: Laurie Aranda
Publishing Coordinator: Iris Sasing
Cover Design: Deb Tremper

Library of Congress Control Number: 2018909188

ISBN: 978-0-6483453-0-5 -- softcover
        978-0-6483453-1-2 -- hardcover
        978-0-6483453-2-9 – ebook (mobi)
        978-0-6483453-7-4 – ebook (epub)
        978-0-6483453-3-6 -- audiobook

Ordering Information:

Quantity sales. Special discounts are available on quantity purchases by corporations, associations, and others. For details, contact the publisher at the address above.

For Media Inquiries, please contact:

STRATEGIES Public Relations
Attn: Jared Kuritz
jkuritz@strategiespr.com
760-550-9850

First Printed in the USA.

DEDICATION

I dedicate this book to you, the reader.

May the inspiration offered here allow you to live from the heart and construct the life of your dreams.

ACKNOWLEDGMENTS

Nothing of value is built in a vacuum. I owe the following people a debt of joyful gratitude for their support and encouragement, not just in the process of writing this book, but in inspiring me to live and lead from the heart.

Thank you to my wife, Marliesa, and my two beautiful children, Myah and Jacob. You are my "why" and the light and inspiration in my life.

Thank you to my family for believing in me and providing the environment of love, trust, and encouragement that allowed me to spread my wings and go for my dreams without hesitation.

I am grateful to Kevin Niv Farrow and the AcuEnergetics® community for helping the world to understand this amazing energy system we all live within and can't live without, demonstrating the profound power of meditation, and aspiring to heal ourselves, each other, and the world.

To the many martial arts instructors and fellow enthusiasts I have met along my journey, thank you for your discipline and dedication to exploring our human potential, and for your personal commitment to demonstrating the physical and mental strength that can be reached through true understanding and right practice.

Thank you to my business mentors, associates, and colleagues for all the tremendous opportunities you have provided to learn, challenge, and grow through so many trials and triumphs along our shared path to success.

Thank you to Brendon Burchard and the High Performance Institute for your dedication and demonstrated excellence in providing an incredible system and community of Certified High Performance Coaching™. You guys ROCK!

Thank you to Helen Chang, Jenny Shipley, and the crack editorial team at Author Bridge Media for their outstanding partnership, professionalism, experience, and expertise in helping me to focus my vision and manifest it into a creation that can be shared with the world. We did it!

I am eternally grateful to my clients, customers, and comrades for providing me with the opportunity, privilege, and honor to spend my days doing what I love and, in doing so, helping us all to stay focused on being of service to others.

Finally, to all those I have listed (as well as any I have forgotten), thank you from my heart to yours for all you have done and continue to do! Your trust, support, friendship, enthusiasm, joy, inspiration, assistance, care, and love are truly appreciated . . . more than you will ever know.

CONTENTS

INTRODUCTION

What matters more than
just what you do by far,
is within every action,
inside how you are.

Struggleville, Population: You

When people ask where you live, you probably give them an honest answer:

Richfield, Minnesota. Or San Diego, California. Maybe Sydney, Australia.

But that's not where you really live. Right now, if you are like most people in this world, you live in Struggleville.

It's not about your physical location. It's about how you feel and where you are mentally.

Let's admit it: you may look very successful on the outside, but inside everything's a mess. Whether in your work environment, with the chaos of running your own business and leading your team, or in your home life, with the challenges of maintaining your household, Struggleville is everywhere.

And everything is out of balance.

Somehow, getting to success has become synonymous with feeling more stress and enjoying life less. You dread going to work. The thought of taking on one more responsibility fills you with panic; you are already under too much pressure as it is. You are not fulfilled, and you are no longer enthusiastic about moving through the seemingly endless steps it will take to get to the next level.

Maybe you have your own business, or you're running a company. Or maybe you're finally leading a team, but you're not sure how to manage it. You've taken every course in leadership and motivation, but you don't have any clarity.

And in the confusion, you may actually be promoting dysfunction. You manage some people one way and other people differently. A new human-resources or management tool comes out, and you try the latest and greatest. It works a little bit, but then it doesn't. And one more idea fades out, leaving only vague, unsettling inconsistency.

Most importantly, you don't feel connected with your team. You're not on the same journey, you're not all engaged, and you're not moving forward together.

It's like you are in separate boats, tied together with ropes, with each person paddling in a different direction. But you believe you are all in one big boat, paddling in the same direction. Some people aren't even in their boat anymore. They've struggled so much that their individual boat has capsized, and now they're sinking. They can't even swim. It's chaos!

You feel the anchor of worry dragging you down, its weight increasing by the day.

You want everyone to be in the same boat, rowing in the same direction. It should be so simple. You know in your heart that your team, your company, your family, and your vision for your life can be so much more than what it is now.

You know you can do better. But how?

Smooth Sailing

There is a way out of Struggleville and into a life of smooth sailing. You can put an end to the constant struggle—and then help others find a more fulfilled life too.

When you have a framework for success, all that stress you've been experiencing is replaced by good health, peace, and clarity. Your struggle is replaced by true, lasting happiness. And the strife caused by living in imbalance is replaced by harmony.

When you implement The BUILD Framework® that I'm going to share with you, you will feel a change—not just philosophically, but also experientially.

With that framework in place, you wake up every day enthusiastic about living *your* life. That enthusiasm propels you to think even bigger than you ever thought you could.

You feel successful on the inside, with a whole new definition of what success really is.

You feel cleaner, lighter, and less burdened. You are empowered. And you have balance.

You amaze even yourself at how far you are able to lead your team members and how simple it can be to guide them to the next level. As you motivate your team members more effectively, they, in turn, re-motivate you.

When your team is connected and working together, you are all in the same boat. And now you've pulled the oars out of the water and strapped an engine onto the back of the boat. You are all in the speedboat of success, and everyone is going to get to the goal exponentially faster. Most importantly, with a warmth in your heart and a smile on your face . . . you actually enjoy the ride!

Can you get out of Struggleville without implementing The BUILD Framework®? Perhaps, if you're lucky. There may be back roads and side roads and secret passageways you can take on your journey, sure.

But I'm building you a highway. And it's one that I— along with lots of other successful people—have driven on. This simple, profound approach will lead you straight to higher levels of personal and professional growth than you could otherwise get to.

The Wake of Ambition

How do I know that you can go from struggling to success—on your terms? Because I've done it, using The BUILD Framework®.

When I struggled the most, outwardly I looked the most successful.

I'd gone from being a childhood prodigy, starring in musicals and other professional performances, to having my own record label. I studied martial arts and law enforcement, going from executive protection to running my own martial arts schools.

One of my best friends, Randy, gave me the opportunity to help him out with his new company, Data Vision. This small start-up was later acquired by The Sabre Group, which spun off to be Sabre; Sabre was subsequently acquired by Electronic Data Systems (EDS). This took me from half a dozen employees at the start-up to 10,000 employees, to 150,000 employees. And just as I thought I had participated in my biggest merger and acquisition experience, along comes Hewlett-Packard (HP) to acquire EDS. This $13.9 billion acquisition was the largest ever in the information technology services sector at the time.

Through each stage of my career, I worked myself out of a job by being a high performer. At each transition, I would rise to the next level. At the end of my time working at HP, I was the head of Global Real Estate for the entire South

Pacific region. Hewlett-Packard had more than 300,000 employees in 160 countries and was doing well over $100 billion in annual revenue. I personally had over 500 team members reporting to me and was responsible for an annual operating budget in excess of $90 million.

Externally, I was successful by any definition. I was making good money. I had a lovely house. I was a fifth-degree black belt and head instructor in my martial arts discipline. I was married to my third wife. And I had a beautiful daughter.

But internally, I had fallen overboard and was drowning in despair.

My wife had made it clear that she no longer wanted to be married, but I wanted to stay anyway, for my daughter's sake. I was repeating a pattern of allowing distance to grow between myself and the relationships I cared about most, then putting up walls when my wife said she was leaving. I didn't want to have three failed marriages.

Although I still loved my work, I wasn't as passionate about it any longer. I could feel the connection to the larger teams I was managing starting to slip.

I didn't have balance.

And I wasn't happy. I didn't have the ability to actually sustain success in my life from the inside out. And I finally said, "Enough is enough."

Enough Is Never Enough

I had already implemented The BUILD Framework® in my corporate gig. Now I realized it could be applied to my life so that I didn't repeat old patterns again—so that I could use the best tools and techniques learned from all my experiences to actually make life better.

Ultimately, I ended up getting that third divorce. That opened me up to meeting the true love of my life, to whom I am now married. And we have a beautiful son together.

Once I took that leap, I also left the corporate environment to start my own company: In Balance with Life. Now I get to work with my wife and help people every single day. Our tag line is "Turning stress, struggle, and strife into health, happiness, and harmony—by embracing the BUILD philosophy." And that is what BUILD has allowed us to do.

I continue with my practice in martial arts and meditation, which has led to a more comprehensive understanding of energetic healing. I became a senior practitioner and meditation teacher in AcuEnergetics®, an amazing healing modality founded by Kevin Niv Farrow in Sydney, Australia. As a teacher of that modality, I was passionate about bringing these ancient teachings to the United States, which I began to do in December 2013.

How did I make sure this was a successful venture? You guessed it. I applied The BUILD Framework®.

As all these things came together, I knew I wanted to go even further in helping other people with my coaching business. I became one of only 200 Certified High Performance Coaches trained by Brendon Burchard from the High Performance Institute.

In my high-performance coaching, my general approach for most clients is to first walk them through Brendon's incredible system. This gives them some of the specific tools and techniques used by the most successful individuals in the world. I then help my clients implement this same BUILD process I'm going to share with you.

These people are surprised and inspired by the simplicity of The BUILD Framework® and how easy it is to have substantial growth in their lives and businesses. Not only do my clients see tremendous success, they actually redefine the meaning of success!

The most important metric for me, at this point in my life and my career, is how I feel. And I feel successful from within the core of my heart. I have a beautiful life, and I'm very grateful for it.

I have found balance.

And now it's my turn to give back. That is the main reason I want to share this life-changing framework with you too.

We're Going to Need a Bigger Boat

What really made me successful in all these arenas, and in obtaining balance, is having The BUILD Framework®. I've had decades of sometimes painful, sometimes joyful—and oftentimes both—experiences. Looking back at my entire journey, I realize my struggles occurred when this framework wasn't in place. And when I was successful, it was because of BUILD.

I used The BUILD Framework® in the corporate environment to run my teams. We actually put the letters B-U-I-L-D up on the walls.

I remember one team that didn't work well when I first came in to the company. The team members didn't get along, they didn't serve their clients well, and they weren't hitting their budget numbers—or any of their other key metrics. Customers were not happy. And we ran all of the facilities and services for Hewlett-Packard in Australia and New Zealand, so we are talking about thousands of customers.

The team members were able to regroup completely using The BUILD Framework®. They went from being viewed as a laughingstock to becoming valued strategic partners with both senior management and rank-and-file employees.

Within thirty days of implementing the BUILD model, we never missed another key metric again. That team hit every single target it was given—and completely turned around the way other executives viewed the whole organization.

In fact, that model inspired others so much that it caught the attention of the person running the entire Asia division. And pretty soon BUILD wasn't confined to just Australia and New Zealand: it had spread throughout the entire region, including Shanghai, Beijing, Taiwan, Hong Kong, Japan, Korea, Singapore, Indonesia, Malaysia, the Philippines, and India.

This massive team of individuals got out of the water and into the same boat—and then we had to get a bigger boat!

Make It Stick

I want you, too, to feel like the captain of your ship: the *Supreme Success*.

This book is unlike any other self-help business book that you've read. Consider it your compass as you navigate out of Struggleville.

You know how with some books you can read the whole thing, but the information just doesn't stick? I don't want that for you. I don't want you to read this book, feel good, and get a little motivated, but then put it down and go back to struggling. If that happens, nothing has really changed. I want this book to help you get out of Struggleville permanently.

I also want the steps necessary to leave Struggleville to be clear and doable. With some books, you gain insight, but figuring out *how* to actually make the lessons stick is hard work.

This book is not hard work.

If you want to struggle, you can do that. If you want to overcomplicate things, go do that. But if you want a simple, straightforward, commonsense approach—with a framework that actually changes your business and your life—then this book is for you.

Take the time to read the whole book, all the way through. During that first read, don't overcomplicate things. Don't worry about trying to remember everything. And don't skip around. The order, and the reason for it, will become clear as you read.

Absorb the information. Give it a chance. Allow yourself to fully read a book—and enjoy the read.

Then read it again. You will realize that once you get it, you *get* it. After reading the book once, you will have the overall context. When you read it a second time, you'll pick up different concepts. You'll read it at a deeper level. Each time through, you'll be able to apply it to your life even more. Take note of what resonates with you.

Keep this book as a reference, but when you are ready, set it aside and start *doing*. This is not just a philosophical conversation about BUILD. I want it to be something you *feel*.

This book is not about learning new tools and techniques. You've done enough of that already. It is about understanding and applying a framework for success. The

BUILD Framework® will allow you to start effectively applying what you've already learned throughout your life.

At the end of most chapters, I have included Action Benefit Challenges—ABCs. These are mini framework exercises that allow you to put the tools and techniques you already know to good use. When you try the ABCs the first time, pick one exercise. The next time you read the book, maybe try to pick three. But keep it simple. Don't try to do a hundred things all at once. Take it one step at a time.

I want you to feel successful. Even more importantly, I want you to feel how the BUILD model can positively influence your life.

A Lasting Transformation

If you are ready to say, "Enough is enough," then you are ready for The BUILD Framework®.

You don't have to settle. You don't have to learn a bunch of different techniques for change. By learning the framework, you take everything you already know and apply it toward changing your business and your life.

And that's what I have to offer you: a lasting transformation from the inside out.

When you use The BUILD Framework® in your business and in your life, you will have the ability to truly feel your success—not just have it, but *feel* it, day in and day out.

And you can't put a price tag on that feeling.

I am really excited to show you how simple this can be. I trust in you and in your confidence and accountability. I'm not taking ownership here; you own your own life. Nor am I guaranteeing any specific results. I can't. Your success is your success. But on the way to that success, know that I absolutely believe in you.

Your journey through BUILD will be different from anyone else's journey, because your life is different. Everyone can apply it differently. I can't promise you the same experience that others have had or will have. This is a standard framework, but the application of it is completely individualized.

I *will* tell you that we can do this together. I know you will enjoy the journey. And I promise to give you a framework that, if you accept accountability and actually apply it, has the potential to transform your life and your level of success. You will have the courage, conviction, and ability to go after your dreams like never before.

Most importantly, you will find balance.

And you will continue to achieve your dreams at a higher, heartfelt level, with meaning and feeling, for the rest of your life.

Are you ready?

Let's BUILD!

Chapter 1

BUILD from the HEART

*Brilliance is not
in complexity found;
keeping things simple,
riches abound.*

Extra Baggage

In April 2010, my third wife and I moved from Dallas, Texas, to Sydney, Australia.

We had to get a shipping container to move all the stuff we had accumulated. And we had to fit everything from our three-bedroom house into that one shipping container. Because it was a corporate move—internationally, no less—movers came to pack everything up. They brought boxes and furniture covers. And they brought big, heavy-duty trash bags to move clothes and soft items like pillows and bedding.

By the time the movers came, we were giving away chairs because they just couldn't fit!

When we got to Australia and the container was delivered, we had to unpack. Opening all the boxes and bags that had been stored in the shipping container was like a reunion with stuff I hadn't seen in months. I never knew what I was going to find. In fact, in one of the big bags, I found garbage—and not just one bag. We had moved three *huge* bags of trash all the way from America to Australia!

When the movers came, they had packed everything. I mean *everything*. We'd had garbage in the garage, so they packed it into bags and sent it along.

After all those discussions and careful decisions about what to take and what to discard, we inadvertently took our lawn trimmings and used coffee grounds with us.

Your Framework File Cabinet

Moving garbage from one country to another was a wake-up call with a hard-to-miss analogy. We all do that in our lives, don't we? Whether it's literally transporting trash, like I did, or metaphorically piling up tools, techniques, and knowledge, we all move crap around with us.

I don't want you to do that anymore! I want you to clean out what is useless, and then make sure you have a place to keep what you need.

Think of this framework as a file cabinet.

You have an abundance of tools and techniques. They are *everywhere*. Some of them are good, and some are not so great. And a lot of them are effective, but only when you know how to use them.

Without The BUILD Framework®, you don't have a place to store these tools and techniques. As a result, you have a really messy desk. And on this desk are your life experiences. Some of the pieces of paper scattered about may contain pearls of wisdom. Other pieces of paper are probably crap and not helpful at all. And maybe others have been dropped onto your desk by other people. But they are all mixed together, because you don't have a system to figure out what to use when and how to easily access it.

With The BUILD Framework®, however, you have a file cabinet with five drawers, in which you can access all the tools and techniques you have learned throughout your entire life. Every single piece of paper goes into one of the five drawers marked B, U, I, L, D—or it gets tossed.

And now your desk is clean! Your file cabinet is full of great stuff you can easily access and use. When a new piece of paper gets placed on your desk, you know where to file it so you can find it again later. Now you can focus on running your business and living your most successful life.

And that expands from you and your specific desk outward to your relationships, your finances, your business— and all the desks that you manage.

With The BUILD Framework®, you will have the ability to manage any of life's challenges that come your way with a totally different outlook. By having a structure in place, you allow yourself to feel more peace and clarity. You will feel lighter. You will find balance. And you will feel more empowered and more productive when everything is in its place—and you know where that place is.

Once the groundwork is laid, everything becomes meaningful and useful to make your life better—in all areas.

BUILD Builds Upon BUILD

As you've probably guessed, BUILD is an acronym:

Build Relationships
Understand the Business
Implement Strategies
Lead and Inspire
Deliver Excellence

And the coolest part about this framework is that BUILD is literally built upon itself. BUILD builds upon BUILD.

But what the heck does that mean, right?

These are not just random letters. They are in this order for a reason. The letter *B* has to come before the letter *U*, not just so we can have fun and spell the word *build*, but because the process for this framework is sequential.

You have to build relationships first so you can fully understand the business. And to really have an idea of how to implement strategies, you must understand the business, which requires the previous step: building relationships. The same is true when you lead and inspire: everything that precedes this step *must* come before it to be effective. Then it all comes together to give you the ability to truly deliver excellence.

You are probably thinking that when you've mastered one letter, you get to sail on through to the next. But nope! At each level, you have to go back to the previous letters; then you'll use that momentum to propel you with greater effectiveness to the next letter and level.

This is a process I call "centrifugal looping." It's like that gravitational force you feel when you are on a ride that spins around and around.

What does that mean here? It means you don't just go B-U-I-L-D. With centrifugal looping, you start with *B*: you build relationships. And then you leverage those relationships to better understand your business: *B-U*. Before you can implement strategies effectively, you have to go back to *B* and look at those relationships you've built—and see if you need to build even more. Then you can understand the business even *better*. And it continues from there.

By the time you loop through delivering excellence, the pattern actually looks like this:

The BUILD Framework®
Centrifugal Looping

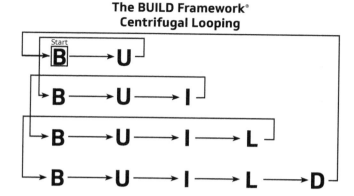

The BUILD Framework® is sequential, tied together in a centrifugal loop. Note that none of the pieces are optional.

For example, in a team environment, every role will use every letter of The BUILD Framework®, but the specific application for each role will most likely be unique. If you put each part of BUILD into a pie chart, the build relationships piece may be 60 percent for you, whereas implement strategies may be only 15 percent. For another role, this may be the opposite: 60 percent implement strategies and 15 percent build relationships.

These numbers will most likely be different for each of your employees. But in each role, *some* percentage will be allotted to each letter. And the total across the BUILD model will be 100 percent in every case.

And it all comes together, throughout the entire framework, in the heart.

A Heart-Based System

From the standpoint of true leadership, everything we're going to talk about is more about feeling than it is about thinking. You already know how to think about your business; that's what has brought you this far. To be more successful, you need to implement The BUILD Framework® from the heart.

That is true for each letter of BUILD.

Relationships are more powerful when they are built from the heart. You may already understand your business in your head—with financial accountability and mastery of what you do—but you can't really understand the business if it doesn't come from the heart. That's a different level, and a much deeper one.

When you implement strategies from the head, you can go out there and get things done. But how does it *feel?* It won't feel right unless you've chosen the *right* strategies, and that comes from the heart. Leading and inspiring? Same thing. You can lead in a very basic way by thinking things through and being philosophical. But if you want to get to the next level of true leadership, ask yourself this question: How does it feel when you're in the zone and people are resonating with you? That's not a thought. It's a feeling!

You will learn to trust that feeling. When you allow your center of gravity to shift from the head to the heart, authentic growth happens. When living from your heart, you can still visit that headspace when necessary to work out the details, but with true leadership from the heart, your understanding of everything deepens.

Finally, delivering excellence is ultimately about being in service to others. You can try to do that from your head—to sell widgets or get clients or chase metrics. But if you don't know how your customers *feel* when you provide a service to them, you're missing the boat.

To help you connect each aspect of BUILD back to the heart, I will include two success attributes in each chapter. These attributes are the specific qualities and virtues you need to apply to each of the individual BUILD letters you work on in order to most effectively discover the profound value and impact of each.

I will also include two emotional contractions, which represent the other sides of those success attributes, working to close you off and block your success in each of the specific areas.

Through experiential awareness of these success attributes and emotional contractions, we can best position ourselves for growth and success. When we understand how these can help and harm, we are more likely to break free from the habitual patterns that hold us back.

I don't want you to struggle and sink into the Lake of Despair any longer. I want you in the BUILD boat. And I want you there with a heartfelt understanding of this system, which will allow you to build your business and your life to the next level of success.

The Ladder to Success

You now know that you have five rungs on the ladder to success as you BUILD from the heart. Those five steps will take your life and your business to the next level.

Build relationships. You will understand whom you and your team need to build relationships with and why. You have limited time, so you want meaningful relationships. How are you going to build those? When you build relationships from the heart, you have authentic relationships built on connections that are open, joyful, and enthusiastic.

Understand the business. You need to know what's driving your business, and you need to learn what you *don't* know so you can leverage the relationships you've built to ask the right questions. It is one thing to understand the business from your head—to know the vision, mission, facts, and figures—but it's another to understand it from a heart-centered perspective, which will allow you to know how it feels and how your business serves your life so you don't struggle anymore.

Implement strategies. Once you understand the business, you will gain clarity about which strategies to implement; this will give you the momentum needed to make progress. Your team members may be able to think of hundreds of strategies, but unless they implement them from the heart, you cannot be certain that what you are doing is actually beneficial. In fact, it may be detrimental. When you implement strategies from the heart, you discover the *right* strategies, which support your greater vision for your life and your business.

Lead and inspire. You can't lead effectively with your head. And you certainly can't inspire. People feel with their hearts, so when you lead with an open heart, people will follow you and get inspired from the feeling you instill within their hearts. Don't be afraid to challenge people and dream big. Leaders lead by leading, not by pulling other people along.

Deliver excellence. Delivering excellence is about putting all these steps together. Ask yourself how your clients *feel* after an interaction with your company. Design the experience for the clients from a feelings standpoint. Understand which behaviors you want to motivate, and measure what matters with meaningful metrics. Be in it for the long game: true excellence is not about quick wins. Reconsider how you define excellence with your center of gravity coming from your heart. When you understand what excellence really means to you, you can make the right decisions and invest the right way for lasting growth.

The next level. Once you've been through the BUILD process, you will learn that the end is actually a new beginning. You will grow throughout this journey, and you'll understand that what comes next is limitless. And you can go out there and do all of it!

With The BUILD Framework® in place, you will get the exponential impact of each piece working together. But if you don't touch all of them, you won't really touch any of them.

Remember that dysfunctional corporate team I was brought in to lead? The team members weren't working well with their customers, and they weren't hitting any of their key metrics.

I introduced the BUILD model at a meeting. I taught the team about the sequential order and how you have to touch all of them. Everyone nodded along and looked inspired to take action.

Imagine my surprise when, after the meeting, one small group of employees told me, "Hey, we're the *B* group. We talk to the customers, so we're the 'build relationships' group."

Another person said, "Yeah, I do the lease work, so I'm in the 'understand the business' group." He pointed to another team member. "And he implements, because he's the guy who actually installs the generators and all that stuff."

The coder in the back room said, "I just do this one thing, so I'm not sure where I belong, but I do know that I don't have to build relationships at all."

They had a whole rationale behind it. And yeah, it made sense, in a twisted sort of way. But from the standpoint of understanding the exponential effect of how BUILD has to work together in balance, it made zero sense. They had missed the entire point.

Once I explained how every person has to touch each letter of BUILD and how it all works together, the team became functional. In fact, it became the team that was brought into the room to help make strategic decisions about the future of the company. And that was all because the team members learned the importance—and the power—of The BUILD Framework®, from the individual level all the way up through the entire organization.

It doesn't matter who you are or what you do. On your BUILD journey, you need to understand each one of these letters—from the heart. Once you do this, you will be able to transform your life into one of lasting success.

And BUILDing from the HEART starts with *B*, which means it's time to build relationships. Chapter 2 shows you how to get started.

Build Relationships

Some time to walk, some time to talk,
some time to just be friends.
Take some time to cherish love;
some time, in time, will end.

Crisis Management

In 2001, I was a regional security manager for Electronic
Data Systems. As the personal liaison to all the federal agencies for my region, I made it my responsibility to know the
teams at the various agencies. If I didn't know them well
enough, I wasn't doing my job.

At the time, a partnership existed between our particular
sector of corporate America and the FBI. We would all go to
lunch once in a while, knowing that we might need to work
together sometime.

I got to know the FBI agents pretty well, and we eventually became good friends. I had them over for game nights.
It's always fun to play Pictionary with the Feds!

On September 11, 2001, when terrorists rammed
planes into the twin towers of the World Trade Center in

New York City, EDS immediately went into crisis mode. We were running the data centers responsible for over 80 percent of the world's travel and transportation systems. These systems held key information, including manifest data containing the individual names of the people on all the planes.

Before the towers even collapsed, people claiming to be FBI agents were calling in to ask for the names of the passengers. I requested the callers leave their names and badge numbers and said I would call right back after verifying credentials.

In the interim, I called one of the FBI agents who had been over to my house the previous week. Let's call him Frank. I didn't call his primary work number; he was flooded with calls too. Instead, I called his personal cell number, which I already had, and he answered right away. Frank was able to tell me that the badge numbers were fake.

The calls were from reporters. Imagine the impact if we had released a list of the passengers on those planes before anyone else knew. Not only would that have severely compromised our response to the crisis, but it also would have been totally inappropriate and callous to broadcast such sensitive information without notifying loved ones first. Can you imagine if you were a family member and found out that way?

If I hadn't known Frank personally, I wouldn't have had anyone to call. With all that was happening on 9/11, do you think Frank would have taken a call from a guy he had met with a handshake five months earlier? Not a chance. But because I had become friends with him, we were collectively able to avoid another mini crisis within the major crisis that had consumed us all.

B Is for Build Relationships

You may never know if or when you are going to need a relationship—not for your own promotion, but in service to others. I could never have understood how important it was to know Frank until it was too late. But because I had built that solid and authentic relationship with him, I was able to deliver the level of service necessary.

When we talk about building relationships from the heart, we are talking about building relationships from a place of authenticity. This is not about counting how many Facebook friends you have. It's about meaningful relationships.

As the first step in The BUILD Framework®, creating these relationships is the foundation for everything to follow.

If you don't get this right, can you still understand the business? Yes, but not as well. Can your team be functional? Sure, but it is on the surface level. People will be cordial. You may have individual stars, but everyone is still in different boats. They're certainly not paddling in the same direction.

When you and your team are engaged in building meaningful relationships—with each other, but also with other key people in your business—it's night and day. People enjoy themselves. They experience the authenticity of true connections.

It is only by understanding the importance of building authentic, meaningful relationships that you lay the groundwork needed to understand the business. That, in turn, lays the groundwork for implementing strategies, leading and inspiring, and delivering excellence.

Building relationships is first in The BUILD Framework®, because it is the most important step to ensure growth and success in your business and your life.

Again, you don't have to be best friends with your employees. You don't even have to be Facebook friends with them. But you do want to sit down with your team and authentically build relationships. When you are present with them, listening to them, you create a connection between yourself and other human beings. This is absolutely necessary if you want to go on to obtain a broader understanding of your business.

Once you understand the importance of building more heart-centered relationships, you need to know three things: whom to build relationships with, why you want to build those relationships, and how you are going to build them. It all starts by being authentic.

Be Authentic

The success attributes that need to be fostered in order to build relationships successfully are patience and relating. If you're patient when relating to someone, you will be able to authentically build that relationship; you are truly connecting with another person.

The emotional contractions that keep us from relating to and being patient with others—thereby halting the relationship-building process—are fear and guilt. When we act out of fear, afraid of what is going to happen or afraid of losing somebody, we tend to do stupid things. If we feel guilty, we cannot relate well, because we're not open, honest, and forthcoming.

Who You Gonna Call?

Once you are open to building personal connections, committing to being relatable and patient, you can put some thought into *whom* you first want to build a relationship with.

Let's not overcomplicate things. Look at the relationships that you know could be important in the business world, or even in your personal life, and choose one to focus on.

I'm not saying you have to stop there. If you have a team of seven people and you've never met with them, meet with all seven. But if you have 5,000 Facebook friends, you're never going to be able to build all those relationships. And most of them probably aren't meaningful anyway.

Make it a priority to ask yourself, "Who is the top person I need to have a relationship with right now for my business?"

When I started one of my new positions at HP, I approached all of the executives, customers, and key stakeholders. Everyone else was afraid to go talk to the managing director and recommended I not try. "No, no, no—he'll call *you* if he wants anything," my coworkers told me.

But I went in anyway. "Hi, I'm JP," I said, hand outstretched. "I'm the director of Global Real Estate. What's going on?"

And he said, "Wow, man, you're the first one from your organization to come and talk to me!"

Now, did meeting this one person later help me understand the business better? You'd better believe it did!

You can do this too. Go to your key stakeholders and ask them, "What are the most important things we're doing for you? What deliverables are we doing well on? Where can we improve?" This is an example of how you can evolve your relationship from basically nonexistent to that of a trusted strategic partner: you build relationships as a foundation to better understanding the business.

Your whole team should be engaged in building relationships, not just you. Every single person in your company needs to build relationships in some way.

And you can't just mandate this, saying, "Now you are all engaged in building relationships!"

That doesn't work. Instead, you can authentically show them the value of building relationships. As you work to make connections with your team members, they will be able to understand the importance of mindful engagement and implement it in their roles—and in their lives.

Now that is one small step that can make a lasting impact.

The Importance of Why

Once you know whom you need to build relationships with, you can identify *why* it is important to build relationships with those specific people.

It is only by asking why that you'll truly understand these relationships. If we don't ask why, we make arbitrary, rather than intentional, decisions about the people around us.

It is important to note that this exercise is not about wanting anything inauthentic. This is not about building relationships to be able to manipulate things to your greater good, or at the expense of others. It's not about faking being friendly with people so you can get what you want by mirroring their behavior or wearing the color shirt that they like. You don't want to use any of those techniques for the dark side, as Yoda might say.

You may be asking, "Well, why not?"

Because it doesn't work. Inauthentic motives always backfire. You can call it karma, universal energy, or just "what goes around comes around," but insincere motivations will come back in a negative way. And that is not building relationships with an open heart.

When we talk about building relationships for yourself and your team, make sure the intention is authentic. Of course, you will find some external and intrinsic value to you; that's why you want to relate to this person. But don't forget the end game is always about being in service to others.

The reason you might want to meet with someone could be because he or she is a key stakeholder. It can be that simple. For example, perhaps you want to meet with the managing director because he or she oversees all the employees in this region, and you provide services to him or her. It's logical to have a relationship with that person.

Keep in mind that your time is limited, and there's only one of you. You or your team can go to dinner with this person or that person, or you can prioritize this call or that call, but you can't do both (at least not simultaneously). So choose wisely, with a clear picture of why a particular relationship is important for you.

Once you know the *why*, you get to have a blast. Don't be stressed; make it fun. What's cooler than meeting other people and authentically connecting with them?

In my book, not much.

Now Is How

You've decided whom you want to build a relationship with, and you know why you want to build that relationship. Okay, great! Now what?

Now you go from thinking about it to putting it into action. Now you decide *how* you are going to build a relationship with the person or people you have chosen.

If you wait until you run into that person, it isn't going to work. You have to take action, and you have to do it now.

This comes back to all those tools and techniques you've learned. What are your tools for building relationships? I'm sure you have several, but here are a few common practices.

First, get it on your calendar. Pick up the phone and call. Or write an email and press "send." Don't think about it anymore; just do it. Then follow up. Get something scheduled on both of your calendars.

Mark off a block of time on your schedule that is used just for building relationships. Then you know exactly when you are going to make those phone calls, send those emails, or schedule those appointments.

Finally, be mindful, and be consistent. This step is not satisfied by running into someone at the coffee shop, talking for five minutes, and then checking the box that says "building relationships."

Building a relationship may mean checking in daily, weekly, or every other week, depending on the relationship. You will usually have more heavy lifting on the front end.

Maybe you schedule half an hour every day for the first few days. Then it's once a week after that. Then maybe it's a monthly catch-up.

I had a lot of corporate relationships like that with key stakeholders. They're busy; you're busy. Gone is the luxury of ample free time for the sake of meeting just to meet. But you're not going to effectively build a strong relationship if you're waiting every month or two to do so. When you build a solid foundation at first, you can maintain it, foster it, and nurture it over time.

I like to think of it like watering a plant. For most plants, you can't ignore them for an entire month and then dump a bucket of water on them as an apology. That's not going to work very well.

Building relationships is the same way. You will learn that some relationships are more like a cactus: you need to nurture them very little, and your time between touch points is much longer. Other relationships, however, are like flowers that need daily attention. Be mindful of what is needed, and you will build successful relationships that allow you both to thrive.

Action Benefit Challenge

Now for the ABCs I promised you'd find at the end of each chapter. You will notice they all follow the same pattern: identify, verify, solidify, and then engage.

In this case, you'll identify one person you need to build or foster a relationship with. Verify why that relationship is important, and then solidify how you can best grow it to the next level. Then engage—go do it!

You can look at the relationships in all areas of your life. Your calendar shouldn't be for just your business. For example, if you want to build a deeper relationship with your wife, do you have a date night on your calendar? Actions speak louder than words, so if it's important to you, plan it.

Diminutive Demands

At the beginning of this chapter, I told you a story that highlighted how important it is to build relationships, even if you don't know at the time how important they might turn out to be. But what happens if you *don't* have those relationships in place? Well, let me share an example of some companies that didn't build relationships.

As the director of security for Sabre, I managed the security operations at all of our data centers worldwide. These centers managed not only the majority of the world's travel and transportation systems, but also many of the online travel agency systems.

While I worked there, somebody was able to hack in and take down one of these major online travel agency systems—just to show us they could. They had our undivided attention, especially when they warned us to get the executives ready: a demand was forthcoming.

I must have watched *Austin Powers* one too many times, because I was expecting the demand to be at least "one million dollars!" But it was $5,000.

You read that correctly; I didn't miss any zeros. Five thousand dollars.

We had been told not to call the cops, but I happened to know an extortion negotiator (remember Pictionary night?). So I quietly invited him into the loop. I knew it was the right thing to do, and the relationship was in place.

Now, your average chief executive officers are probably walking around with $5,000 in their pockets, right? And the company definitely had petty cash or expense accounts to cover that amount. This was something we could pay. But the dollar amount wasn't the point.

The point was that we had the relationships in place to dig deeper. Ultimately, we discovered that these same people had been doing this on an ongoing basis, hitting about ten companies a day for $5,000 each . . . and they'd been getting away with it for more than six months! Even if these people worked only on business days, they were making $1 million a month.

Nobody else had bothered to report it. Why? The amount was only $5,000. Those other companies just paid and figured the hackers would go away. And they did—right on to the next company that didn't care enough about paying such a small amount.

The point is, those other companies hadn't built relationships with authorities who could help, so reporting these strange demands was more hassle than it was worth. Each company paid the money without resisting, and the extortion stayed undetected. But that was the wrong decision. Eventually, the hackers hacked the wrong company when they hacked us—the ones who had built the right relationships first.

Even if nothing this dramatic ever happens to you or your company, it is beneficial to have those relationships in place. And you can't take the next step—understanding your business—until you build relationships. Chapter 3 builds upon this first step to show you just that: how you can better understand your business for greater success.

Understand the Business

*The thing you really need to know
to make your dreams come true,
is that you'll always need to grow
into the dream that's you.*

Ivy Davis

One of my first jobs after high school was as a floor detective at Target. This was back in the days before they had the surveillance cameras they have now. I was part of the loss prevention team—in charge of stopping shoplifters—at the store on Lake Street in Minneapolis.

I'll never forget Ivy Davis, our trainer. She was around eighty years old, and a lot of people assumed she was too old to teach us anything. But she was amazing! And she was a wealth of information.

Ivy had great surveillance techniques, and she had the best arrest record in the region to go along with them. I chose to walk the rounds and grab a cup of coffee in the Target Café with her as much as I could, because she obviously knew something none of the rest of us did. The most important thing I learned from Ivy was the ability to hide in plain sight. I still remember hearing her say, "Don't assume they think you're security."

No one in a million years would think this little old lady was part of the loss prevention team. Shoplifters would take merchandise right in front of her!

Back then, VHS tapes cost like $80, and they weren't locked up yet; they were right out on the shelves. And shoplifters would just pick them up and stuff them in their bag or down their pants, right in front of Ivy! But she understood that shoplifters assumed everyone around them was scrutinizing them, so she would relax and act casually, all the while calling in backup to help with the actual takedowns.

And because I learned to be so comfortable with Ivy's approach, I became one of the best floor detectives too—all part of understanding the business of how to catch shoplifters.

U Is for Understand the Business

At the time, I had no idea that what Ivy was teaching me would fit into The BUILD Framework®. But while I was learning new surveillance techniques and building my relationship with my mentor, I was also deepening my understanding of the business.

Understanding and learning are really the same. In order to understand the business, you must have the ability to constantly learn. As you learn, you will grow into a person who can achieve the level of success you dream of. And you continue growing and evolving through understanding your business.

If we don't know what our businesses are doing, we are doomed. If we don't seek to understand business and life more fully, we are certainly not going to have the level of success we could otherwise have. And if your team members don't understand the business at a deeper level, they might be performing and doing okay, but they aren't contributing to the exponential growth that is possible.

When your team members are curious about the greater collective, they are learning at an increased capacity. They understand the connection between what they do individually and what the team is doing as a whole. It is only when we have that curiosity in life—to continue learning and seek to understand what we are doing, whether in life, in business, or with our families—that we find success in every aspect of our lives.

Strive with curiosity to understand your own life better. Once you understand yourself, you can seek to understand others. And that understanding will help you have a stronger connection to your team, which circles back around to building a stronger understanding of your business. Growth comes from taking the time to understand what you are curious about and then building upon that curiosity to strengthen your knowledge.

Don't forget that *U*, understanding the business, is built upon *B*, which is building relationships. The more you form sound, authentic, deep relationships—both in your life and in a business context—the more you'll be able to leverage those relationships to understand the business. And again, the better you understand the business, the stronger foundation you are laying for implementing strategies, leading and inspiring, and ultimately delivering excellence.

In order to understand the business, you need to start by being curious. Then you can learn what you don't know by asking questions and listening with your heart. An important step in this process is knowing where to draw the line when further knowledge is actually unnecessary and a waste of your time.

Be Curious

The success attributes for understanding the business are nurturing and learning. You must literally nurture your learning potential in order to truly understand anything.

The emotional contractions are overcontrol and hanging on, or not letting go. When we are overly controlling and insistent on trying to do things our way, we are not able to learn. And when we hold onto our opinions or the way we've always done things, we don't have the capacity to learn.

To learn new things, you must loosen your grip of control and let go with openness and trust. When you let go and genuinely want to learn from others—with a connection to the heart—your understanding grows.

Know What You Don't Know

At this point in life, you've probably realized you don't know everything. There's always more to learn. But before you go running around trying to learn everything at once, stop. Be still. And then take stock of what you *don't* know—but should.

You don't need to know just your thirty-second elevator speech—though you should know that. What you do need to know as leader of your team, company, or business is what additional information you require for a more complete understanding of your business.

When I was in my last corporate gig, I was asked to run the Global Real Estate service delivery organization for the South Pacific region. Prior to that, my operational background was primarily in security services. I had no clue about real estate service delivery. My knowledge was basically at the level of "Do the lights work? Okay, then it looks good!"

I had no idea about lease rates and owning versus buybacks and all this stuff. So what did I do? I talked to a lot of people, and I started to build those relationships. And

I used them to help me figure out what I needed to know. My centrifugal loop led me back to *B* before I could move once again on to *U*—understand the business, this time at a deeper level.

Then I made charts and flash cards for each location under my new scope. These cheat sheets outlined specifics such as head count, square footage, power utilization, key stakeholders, building management systems, lease dates and rates, and all of the acronyms I needed to know in case the CEO of HP asked the VP of GRE how JP's OPEX, CAPEX, and SLAs in SP were doing. (Whew, that was a mouthful!)

I learned every detail because it was important—and because I was curious. I was being paid to lead that region, which required understanding the business. I was being paid to know it well enough that I could successfully implement strategies in a way that led and inspired, allowing our team and, ultimately, the company to deliver excellence.

So many people don't learn anything outside of their immediate roles because they are paralyzed by fear. And that fear is often due to imposter syndrome: feeling like a phony because you don't know something you think you should. If you feel that way, then take the time to ask questions and go learn whatever it is you need to know. If your team members feel like imposters, encourage them. Have them role-play with one another and challenge each other to learn and grow.

Until you know the areas where you have gaps in your knowledge, you won't know what questions to ask—or whom to ask.

Ask Questions and Listen with Your Heart

Once you know what you don't know, how do you gain that knowledge? You ask questions!

Don't wait for someone to ask if you want to know something. Focus on understanding the things you don't know, and then, among the relationships you have developed, figure out the right people to ask for help. Trust they will answer your questions honestly when you unflinchingly ask, "What are the things I should know?"

When I was the director of global operations for the Chief Security and Privacy Office at EDS, I brought all the regional managers—from all over the world—together from time to time. At one such gathering, we had a forum during which people gave presentations about their individual parts of the business.

One of the presentations was given by the global leader of investigations, who happened to be from Texas and who was fond of the term "y'all." In her presentation, she said things like "Y'all will do this. Y'all will do that."

As she spoke, I noticed that the manager from India, who was very astute and usually wrote everything down, stopped writing and sat back with a smile. He didn't write another word throughout her entire presentation.

During the break, he came up to me and said, "JP, I want to thank you for an amazing forum. I have just two questions: Who is Y'all, and when can I meet him? It sounds like he's going to do all the stuff I thought I would be doing!"

Inside, I was cringing. I had to tell him that "y'all" was slang for "you all," and that he would be doing those tasks after all. We gave him the notes from the speech and learned a big lesson: don't assume others are hearing the same thing you are. Ultimately, though, that manager from India was able to learn what he didn't know by asking follow-up questions, even when the answer was unexpected.

Don't be afraid to ask your questions. Whatever you are uncomfortable with, ask about that so you can understand it better. And do it with an open heart.

Asking questions isn't useful in the understanding process if you don't listen to the answers. In order to understand your business, you need to truly listen—not just hear what people are saying.

Hearing is just with the ears. Listening is with the heart. It occurs deep inside you. So don't just hear. *Listen.*

You are going to learn and understand more when you ask questions and listen with true humility. If you ask merely because you think you should, you aren't open to learning. But when you ask and truly listen, you will get the subtleties that help you understand what's actually happening with your business.

Finally, encourage your team members to ask questions too, even—or especially—about something that makes them uncomfortable. Make it clear that *everyone* needs to understand more about the business. Have each person ask one question about a part of the business that's unfamiliar or puzzling. Then have someone in that department answer the question so you can all learn together.

No one needs to become a subject matter expert in every aspect of your entire company; that's unreasonable. But encourage curiosity, and it will be instilled in all of your team members.

Know Where to Draw the Line

One of the most important concepts in understanding the business is learning where to draw the line and say, "Okay, I know enough," or "I can look that up."

In AcuEnergetics®, we learn about the traditional Chinese medicine acupuncture points on the body—hundreds of them. But do I really need to memorize them all? No. I can look them up in the Deadman's Acupuncture Manual on my desk.

The same is true in your business. There will be things you simply don't need to know that you or your team can look up. Understanding that limit prevents you from wasting your valuable time trying to cover every base.

I had to learn a similar lesson—to understand what I know and be willing to accept a certain level of risk—when I ran global security operations for data centers. At the time, we had "red teams" that were authorized to plan how to break in and take down a data center. Those drills showed us the potential weak spots in our security and guided the design of new protective strategies that would safeguard the data.

Our data center was significantly secure: it was underground, with cameras, motion detectors, and a host of additional technologically advanced bells and whistles. The red team had a hell of a time coming up with a plan that could possibly compromise our center.

After much thought (and apparently too many action movies), the team members reported they had discovered a hole in the system and proceeded to describe it: "If we get a helicopter, rappel down into one of the cooling towers, cut the grate, and get in underneath, avoiding the fan blades, you are exposed."

I just looked at them. "I'm okay with that risk."

I wasn't going to redesign the entire cooling tower because the red team members had conceived a plan that gave them the slimmest of chances to work their way in. Now, if they had said, "The front door is unlocked, no one is there, and we just walked in and hit the power off button," then we would want to take a closer look.

But because I understood the business, I also knew when I didn't need to know more. It is possible to be a professional student forever, locked in a room studying, never moving forward and engaging because you are not satisfied with the level of knowledge you have obtained.

Action Benefit Challenge

Your ABC now is to identify one area in the business that you don't understand as well as you should.

Once you've chosen the one thing you need to understand better, ask yourself, "Why do I need to understand that?" If you are genuinely curious and want to know more, great! But if it doesn't pass the *why* threshold, throw it out. Don't do it just for something to do.

Next, solidify *how* you are going to learn the needed information. Ask anyone you need to ask—build that relationship if you need to—and truly listen to the answer. Have a conversation. Create flash cards. Use whatever tools and techniques you have at your disposal to learn what you need to.

Now get it done!

First Date Flash Cards

Outside of your business, take a look at your relationships. Remember that you work to live—you don't live to work.

And if you don't understand the business of marriage, watch out!

In the same way, you have to know what you don't know. What are the things you don't know that are meaningful to you or your partner? What's on your flash cards? Maybe it's his birthday, your anniversary, her favorite flowers, or the first time you kissed.

The point is not how much time you spend understanding the business of your life, but ensuring you are fully engaged with heartfelt curiosity in taking your life to a deeper level. When you understand that this is what's most important—not just making money and providing for your family—it's like magic! The business of raising a family and/or nurturing personal relationships is the business of *life*.

When you more fully understand the business of all areas of your life, your marriage, and your relationships, you'll advance to the next level of growth, both personally and professionally.

Now you know what you don't know about understanding your business and what to do with this knowledge. What's next? It's time to take action! In chapter 4, you will learn how to implement strategies to bring even more success into your life.

Chapter 4

Implement Strategies

Throughout the wisdom of all time,
no matter what you've heard,
a fact remains that is the same—
actions speak louder than words.

Join Now! It's about to Start!

You've probably seen websites advertising live webinars. An eye-catching message on the home page urges you to act: "Hurry, join now! It's about to start!"

If you click through, you learn that 282 people are registered for the webinar. "Only three seats left!" you are warned.

The number of available seats counts down as you join. You can see chats and comments with time stamps scrolling on the screen: "Two minutes left . . . One minute left . . . Your webcast is starting now!"

But it's not real.

That content is a recording. It's always up there, and it plays automatically when you click on it. The chats are fake.

Even the countdown timer is staged. It's not a webinar; it's a fake-inar.

And people actually buy it.

Some people will assure you that everyone knows it's fake. Regardless, these marketers go through a lot of effort to fake out potential participants. Why? Because it's been proven that people are more likely to join if other people are there. The value of that supposedly "live" webinar comes from its audience. Even if customers figure out the deception, they've already become a customer, so the marketers don't care.

But why would they want to get customers that way?

I'm not against using technology to increase your business sales and share your brand more broadly. My point is that it's better to be clear and honest—and not manipulative by deception.

I Is for Implement Strategies

As you can see, some strategies look good on paper. After all, marketing techniques like the one I just described are out there because they work. But if they don't feel right—if they aren't authentic, and if they don't connect with the heart—then they aren't the right strategies to implement.

You have built some relationships. Then you worked toward understanding the business. Based upon that deeper understanding, you probably had to loop back around and ask yourself, "What other relationships do I need to have?" Then you built those relationships to understand the business even deeper. And now you are propelled forward, because it's with the understanding you have—based upon the relationships you have formed—that you have a much better idea of what strategies to implement.

You can probably already see that when you do this again, you are going to get to truly lead and inspire. Why? Because no one else is doing this! That's the brilliance and importance of implementing the right strategies.

The key word here is "implement."

Implementing strategies is about action. It's about getting stuff done. This part of The BUILD Framework® is not thinking about or researching strategies; it's about implementing them to get traction and movement, whether that's in your business or your life.

So many people get stuck thinking about strategies. They have all these ideas about what they could do, or how to market this way or that, or how to expand their service offerings.

"I think I'll build a website," they say.

And that's great. But when you ask them, "What have you actually done?" the proverbial crickets chirp. They can't answer.

It's better to pick one strategy and actually implement it than to think about half a dozen you never start.

Can you arbitrarily fall into doing things and sort of fake your way into some strategies for a while? Yeah, maybe. But we're talking about implementing strategies in a mindful way, because that is what leads to lasting success.

To implement strategies that connect with the heart, you want to start by doing it right, then implement the *right* strategies, take action, and be flexible.

Do It Right

The success attributes for implementing strategies are discernment and will. Discernment means knowing what to do and making the right decisions. Will is necessary to show up as your best self each and every day and to do what you know is right.

When you have discernment and will based in the heart, you can implement strategies effectively at a level above and beyond anything you can imagine.

The emotional contractions that stop us from being able to implement strategies effectively are worry and dishonor. When we're worried all the time, we often stop ourselves from taking necessary risks.

Or if we're doing something dishonorable—if we implement strategies that do not have that connection to the heart—then those strategies are the wrong ones to pursue.

Implement the *Right* Strategies

I can hear you asking already, "So what strategies are my team and I supposed to implement?"

I can't answer that specifically, because I don't understand *your* unique business. But I can tell you generally that you are going to implement the *right* strategies. And that comes down to understanding how those strategies feel. If a strategy feels authentic, open, and amazing, then—as they say in Australia—Bob's your uncle!

I have a martial arts background, and the word "right" has deeper connotations in that world. It is part of a samurai code that means much more than just doing the right thing. One of the practices of the samurai from ancient times was literally stepping through doorways with their right side first. Why did they do this? On a surface level, it was because they wanted to put their strong side first, so they were prepared to counter an attack.

But in martial arts—as in life—there is always a deeper meaning. On a deeper level, this practice represented the aim to always have one's full awareness on "right" when transitioning, not just from one room to another, but during all transitions in life.

Now, your business probably isn't under threat of being attacked. And whether you decide to step into every room with your right foot or not, you can be mindful of leading with the intent of always doing right.

When you implement a strategy, you want it to be authentic, straightforward, and heartfelt. You want your team to implement strategies with integrity. You want to do it right.

If you want to know if a strategy is the right strategy, ask yourself this: "How would I feel if everything I did with this strategy was on the front page of the newspaper, with total transparency?"

If the answer is anything other than "I'd feel 100 percent fine with that," pause and ask yourself why you are implementing that strategy.

Being mindful about what strategies to implement goes back to understanding the business. You are mindful because you understand that, sure, you can do something that may not feel right, and in the short term, you might get some positive results. But if it's not the right strategy, then you risk damaging your brand and creating a reputation of being inauthentic.

This is not leading with right. This is not the way of the samurai. This is not the way to true success.

Take Action

The second part of implementing strategies, after you choose strategies that are right for you and your team, is to take action. Actions speak louder than words, so what are your strategies telling your team, your company, and your clients?

If you and your team are not taking action, you may be thinking that you're not saying anything at all. Actually, inaction can do the opposite. It sends a clear message that you may be disengaged, apathetic, or unwilling to be bothered.

In the corporate world, we tend to get analysis paralysis at times: we want to make everything perfect before we act. But often what we are really doing is second-guessing ourselves. And then we stall out.

Sometimes implementing strategies can be as simple as putting a policy in place—immediately.

When I was running global data center security operations for Sabre, we never had any issues with children in our data centers. Do you know why? Because children weren't allowed.

Before we put that policy in place, we were approached each quarter by schools and other organizations requesting tours. After all, these were some of the coolest facilities in the world, with bomb blast doors, weight booths, iris scans—more advanced and more awesome than any movie out there.

After each request, a review committee would form to labor over each decision. We never approved the requests, because it never made sense. Many years back, one tour had been approved, but the requests kept funneling in, every single quarter.

The same day I heard about this, I met with a few of the other executives, and we enacted a policy that put the entire issue to rest immediately. That action took less than two hours. Moreover, the dozens of hours spent processing these requests could now be focused on more important tasks.

How many issues do you currently have that can be solved by putting some simple policies in place?

You want to instill courage in your team members, empower them to implement the strategies you have decided upon, and take action with authenticity and from the heart.

Will your strategies always be perfect? Of course not. Your team is going to stumble sometimes, and you are going to encounter peaks and valleys. But you will be moving. Your team will be engaged and excited and will continue the momentum.

Once your team members understand the concept of implementing the right strategies, they will work together to create the perpetual action that propels you onward to even greater success.

Be Flexible

Finally, when you're implementing strategies for yourself and your team, be flexible.

I am certified in the Reid Technique of interviews and interrogations, the same training utilized by the FBI and other law enforcement agencies around the world. Reid is all about obtaining *truthful* confessions, not just getting people to confess. I like this technique because it is used by those who are driven by integrity.

Reid has nine steps, which include proposing an alternative question at step seven to obtain a truthful confession. But sometimes people get so tied up in the specifics of this strategy that they lose their flexibility and miss the whole point.

For example, during one high-profile case, an investigator was only on step three when the suspect started to confess. The aim of the technique is to get to the truth—and if the truth is that the suspect is guilty, to get a confession.

This particular investigator, however, was so locked into the process that he could not see what was happening right in front of him. He was actually saying to himself, "No, no, no. I don't want a confession yet. I haven't proposed the alternative question!"

Implementing strategies is important, but so is having some flexibility to adapt those strategies when necessary.

Remind your team never to forget the end game: delivering excellence. If you have a team member who implements a strategy to close a sale, he or she should recognize when that sale is closing, even if it's in the middle of the pitch. You don't want a customer to call you up, ready to buy the product, but then be halted by an employee who says, "No, you have to go back through the funnel. That's how I sell things."

If the client wants to give you money, that's the end game! Empower your team members with the knowledge and flexibility to stop what they are doing and accept the sale.

And it's in the doing of it—in implementing the strategies—that you get that additional information, which builds momentum and evolves into new, even better strategies.

Action Benefit Challenge

The ABC for implementing strategies is pretty straightforward. In fact, you may have already guessed it. Figure out one strategy that you want to implement. What can you do right now, this quarter? Not next quarter, not next year, not when you get around to it. What can you do now? And what can you do to foster this environment of implementing strategies for your team?

After you identify that strategy, ask yourself why the strategy is important to you and your business. Verify why this is the *right* strategy for you. Then solidify exactly *how* you are going to get this done. Dust off the Gantt charts and other project management tools if appropriate.

Now get out there and go do it! If you really want to leave a legacy, make a mark, and find true success, then you have to finish what you start. You have to get it done.

The AWESOME Life Club

In early 2017, I decided I was going to start a Facebook group called The AWESOME Life Club. I knew I had a strong, heartfelt message, and I wanted to get it out there and share it with the world.

Instead of looking at simply gaining a swarm of members, my focus was on how to provide value. I had tons of creative ideas in this space, but that didn't matter. What mattered was turning those ideas into action.

I built out the AWESOME acronym (of course it's another acronym!): Awake, Wondrous, Engaged, Still, Open, Meaningful, and Energized. *Awesome* has seven letters, and there are seven days in a week, so every day I ask a question that corresponds to one of those seven qualities.

Next, I came up with original inspirational quotes like those you've seen at the beginning of each chapter. I posted those consistently, every week. And each week, I did a deeper dive on my blog to explain the meaning of the quote. I understood the business of having an awesome life!

From the day we launched The AWESOME Life Club, those quotes, questions, and pictures went up—every day of the week. Could I have spent more time agonizing over whether each question was absolutely perfect? Fretting about which quotes to use? Sure. But then I wouldn't be any further along than I was that first day.

The membership count of The AWESOME Life Club is now in the thousands—and it's growing all the time! This organic growth gives me a platform, which allows me to lead and inspire—and, ultimately, deliver excellence.

Now you know how your strategies can go deeper and mean more than ever before. But your action doesn't stop there: it's time to lead and inspire! Chapter 5 will show you the way.

Chapter 5

Lead and Inspire

It might be fine for what it is.
True vision is to see . . .
How, in time, what is becomes
what can truly be.

Karate Kid

When I started that job in loss prevention at Target, which I told you about in chapter 3, I was also just starting martial arts. I was about halfway to black belt, so while I knew some techniques, I definitely wasn't a master of anything. But that training came in handy for arresting shoplifters.

One day, a huge guy with the physique of an American football player came into my store. He loaded up televisions, video tapes, and electronic razors in a cart, even stuffing some items in his jacket, and headed out the front door. I flashed my badge at him, and he didn't even slow down.

This guy pushed the cart full of stolen merchandise straight at me and then took off running across the parking lot.

I couldn't think of what to do, so I sprinted after him. "Holy crap! I'm going to have to fight this guy. And he's big!" I remember thinking to myself. I'm not big now, and I was only eighteen at the time.

After a few minutes of running, I could tell the guy was getting tired because I was gaining on him. He started crossing the street on the far side of the parking lot, but he stopped on the median, scooped up a big stick, and turned around, ready to fight. Dozens of people were watching.

I decided to psych him out.

I did a Superman dive through the air, tucked and rolled, and came up to do three 360-degree fan kicks. Then I stood in position, just like in the *Kung Fu* movies, ready to fight—or be killed.

And this guy dropped his stick, fell to his knees, and pleaded, "Don't hurt me, Karate Kid!"

I cuffed him and walked him back to the store. My nickname from that point on was Karate Kid. And no one ever messed with me again!

L Is for Lead and Inspire

That day, I learned that sometimes you have to be the person you didn't even know you could be. For me, that person was a martial arts expert, even though I had yet to become one. For you, that person could be a true leader—even though you may have yet to become one.

You've done all the rest of it—building relationships, understanding the business, and implementing strategies.

Leading and inspiring is where you step up and get to the next level of The BUILD Framework®—not just for yourself, but for your team. It is about actually changing your practices to become your best selves. Together, you all perform at a higher level, with a heartfelt connection.

In the business world, you may come across a lot of people doing their own things. And you are going to see a lot of egos. Both of these can lead to poor interactions with others, which leads to a bad work environment.

You, as a leader, set the tone at the top. The way you run your company, your team, or your life will cascade throughout everything you do—and it will touch everyone you work with. If you embody exactly the kind of behavior, thinking, and attitude you want to see from your team members, guess what? They are going to reflect it back.

Become the change you want to see—not just in yourself, but in those around you—and you will inspire that growth. This is true leadership.

To lead and inspire from the heart, you have to dream it and be it, then dream even bigger, push yourself, and lead with unity.

Dream It, Be It

The success attributes for leading and inspiring are recognition and giving. With recognition and giving, you have the clarity to see what contributions need to be made and the ability to share them with others.

The emotional contractions that stop you from being able to lead and inspire effectively are overconcentration and anger. When we are in our heads all the time, our attention and energy are focused inward, in a contracting manner. This diminishes our ability to lead because it blocks our ability to accurately view life with an open perspective. When we are angry, we block giving and kindness. And we can't lead and inspire by being angry. We only truly lead and inspire by allowing our hearts to expand outward.

Dream Big, Lead Bigger

The first step to lead and inspire is to dream it.

Whenever I explain this to people, they inevitably ask me, "Shouldn't I dream it *before* I implement strategies so I know what to do?"

But the answer is no. This "dream it" comes after "do it right" on purpose, because you need the momentum that is building. It is only after implementing strategies that you can truly lead and inspire, because you have to do great things—not just think about them. If you haven't done anything, you haven't gone anywhere, so there is nowhere for people to follow.

Once you've implemented strategies, you are in a position to lead and inspire. So *now* dream it! And dream big.

If you want to reach 10,000 people with your message, then multiply that by 10 and make it 100,000!

Then be it. Live it. You are preaching this stuff, so you have to live it. You can try to fake it, but that won't get you very far. It's like that fake webinar we talked about earlier. Faking it may seem to work in the short term, but eventually it's exposed as a farce. More importantly, you are the one who has to look at yourself in the mirror every day. You can't fake your way through feeling uncomfortable with how you live.

If you're not really engaged in doing what you ask your team members to do, they are going to feel it. And when you *are* engaged, they're going to feel that, too. You will make a much greater impact because your confidence and understanding will be so much higher.

Your integrity to lead your team members is so much stronger when you are living exactly what you want them to be. True leadership comes when you embody your dreams yourself and then inspire others to follow.

Most importantly, remember that you set the tone at the top.

For you as a leader, it's not just about the words you say; it's about your actions, too. If you ask your team to be in the office from nine in the morning until five at night, but you stroll in at ten and leave at three, you have a disconnect in how you lead and what you want to inspire.

If you want a culture of embracing openness and working together, then it's up to you to demonstrate those behaviors. Because you are always leading. You're always influencing. You can't opt out of leadership. The question is not "*Do* you want to influence?" but rather "*How* do you want to influence?" If you need a break, take a day off. But when you're the leader, remember that everyone is watching.

So what will allow you to lead and inspire more effectively? First, dream it. What is your vision for your company? What is the vision for your employees? Do they share that vision and really feel it? Then be it. Put that vision into practice. Inspire your employees by practicing it daily.

When you lead and inspire at every level, your entire team can follow you to success.

Push Yourself

In leading and inspiring, you also have to push yourself.

When I was eleven years old, I landed the lead role in the world premiere of Dr. Seuss's *The 500 Hats of Bartholomew Cubbins* at the Minneapolis Children's Theatre.

I memorized all my lines, rehearsed every day, and attended all the dress rehearsals. I was as ready as I'd ever be. But I had never performed in front of a full house.

On opening night, more than 750 people were in attendance, including Theodor Geisel, Dr. Seuss himself. A full orchestra played the overture. The lights went black.

The spotlight was going to come up any second, and I was supposed to be on stage, sitting on a tree stump ready to sing.

And I froze. I couldn't for the life of me go out there.

But Wendy Lehr, who played my mom, whispered, "Go!" and shoved me onto that stage. I went sprawling.

When the lights came up, though, I was sitting on that tree stump. The audience erupted into applause. I felt their energy, and I was fine. In fact, I was better than fine. I knew I could do it. And I never missed a line.

Now, you probably don't have someone shoving you onto a stage. But who is pushing you? Who is pushing your team?

Meg Whitman, the former CEO of HP, enacted a policy when she worked there to really push her team to do everything she knew it could—and more.

When she took over, the overwhelming feedback from customers was that things were taking too long. So she implemented a new policy: "Escalate in 24 hours and resolve in 48 hours." This meant that if a problem wasn't resolved, it would be escalated within 24 hours. And no matter what that problem was, it would be resolved within 48 hours. No exceptions.

When she first shared this policy, I'm sure she had no idea if the whole company could *really* live up to those standards. But she set the expectation. It was her moon shot, just like when former US President John F. Kennedy said we were going to send a man to the moon—and return him safely to Earth.

How many people did those two statements motivate and push? At HP, the entire company. With the moon landing, the whole nation—and then the entire world.

What is your moon shot? How can you push your team—and yourself—to be even better?

Find those moments where you can lead and inspire, even if you have to push yourself a little harder to set outrageous expectations. Trust that it will be okay, and allow it to happen. And push to be your best self so you can inspire and lead others to the next level.

Lead with Unity

You can't lead others if no one is following. You not only need to lead; you need to lead with unity.

One of the senior vice presidents I reported to in the corporate context taught me a trick to always lead with unity. That trick is three *D*s and an *A*.

I learned that when the door is closed—when you are with your team, or when you are with other leaders—you are going to do the three *D*s: discuss, debate, and decide. In that room, you welcome every different opinion your team has. And you can discuss it and debate it until the cows come home. But you don't leave that room until you get to the third *D*, which is decide.

Once that decision is made, you have the *A*: act in alignment. When that door opens, no one should be able to tell who thought what—not other people in the company, and certainly not your clients. They will know only what you all decided. And you will all be on board, in alignment.

When you act in alignment with your team, you have the ability to cultivate a collective pride of ownership. You may have debated fiercely, but you made an agreement. And then you all share it. Each team member should be able to articulate the decision as if it were his or her own.

Nothing will kill the morale of a corporation faster than one person going to his or her team and saying, "Well, I guess we're going to go down this path. I don't want to; I think it's the stupidest decision ever made. But you know what? I have to do it, so you have to do it. Good luck!"

That's not inspiring. That attitude doesn't help the company. It is the opposite of effective leadership.

When your team is comfortable with The BUILD Framework®, will you still have differences of opinions? Sure. And you'll want to foster open communication and the sharing of ideas, creating the opportunity to discuss and debate as appropriate.

However, with BUILD, everyone will have an increased ability to ultimately buy in to the strategies you are implementing with authenticity. And you will lead them, in unison, to achieve your goals.

Action Benefit Challenge

Your ABC for leading and inspiring is to ask yourself, "What are the ways in which I can be pushed?" Identify that one thing you know you need to go out there and do.

Then verify that this is the right thing to do, given all your options.

Now solidify your plan for how you are actually going to make this happen, and write it down.

Then go do it! Do you need to book a speaking engagement? Then literally push yourself out there on that stage! Call a nonprofit organization; they are often looking for speakers.

Whatever it is, start doing it. Other people will notice you are doing more and will be inspired. You lead by example, so start leading!

That Guy

When teaching about leading and inspiring, I always say to "be it." But be careful so you don't become the guy you *don't* want to be.

My wife and I recently decided to start a vegan diet, which means we don't eat any animal products. Prior to that, I drank a flat white coffee (coffee with milk) every day. So when I went to the coffee shop, my wife told me, "You can have almond milk, coconut milk, or soy milk. But make sure it's GMO-free."

I went up to the counter to order and saw a new guy working there. He looked at the cash register like it was the controls to a spaceship.

"Is your soy organic?" I asked.

"Huh?" He just looked at me.

I repeated myself. "Your soy milk. Is it organic?"

He looked at me blankly again and then handed me the box of soy milk. "I don't know. Read this."

I could tell the line behind me was getting longer and longer. I could *feel* the breath of the woman behind me on my neck.

There's no way I was going to take the time to read this whole box. I didn't even know where the ingredients were listed! I just said, "Yeah, okay. That's fine. Thanks."

I finally got my soy milk flat white, and I turned around to see a line out the door. As I walked out, I heard an older woman whisper to her friend, "He's a vegan!"

When you lead and inspire, be careful that you don't become the person you don't want to become. For a moment there, I became *that* guy who holds up an entire coffee shop just to read the label on a box of soy milk!

You have completed the first four steps of BUILD, and now you have only one step left: the step that all others lead to, the step where it all comes together. The next chapter will show you how to deliver excellence.

Chapter 6

Deliver Excellence

No matter how you serve this world,
inside may you have pride.
And may you never once forget
the value of the vibe.

The Gumtree Good Deed

One of my clients, Andrew, was selling a big leather chair on Gumtree, which is an online classified ads site—basically, the Australian version of Craigslist in the US.

He really wanted this chair to go to a good home because it was one of those motorized chairs that help push you into a standing position. He didn't need it anymore, but he knew it would be perfect for someone else who might really need that assistance.

He had spent over $1,000 on it, and it was still in great condition, so he listed it for $500.

A few guys had stopped by to see the chair and asked if Andrew would take anything less than $500. Andrew could tell these guys didn't really want the chair: they wanted a bargain so they could resell the chair for a profit. He didn't budge. The price was still $500, he told them.

Another guy saw the ad, drove a long way to come see the chair, and wanted to buy it. "Oh, it would be perfect for my wife!" he told Andrew. "She can't stand up easily because she has a medical issue, and this would really help her."

He had been looking for something like this for a long time, but he hadn't been able to find one he could afford. And his story was heartfelt and genuine.

He was worried about how to get it back to the truck he had borrowed—he couldn't lift it on his own—and then he started counting out the money he had in his wallet, down to his very last dollar. He counted it twice. He looked at Andrew and asked, "Is there any way you could accept anything lower than $500? I only have $475."

"How about this?" Andrew replied. "Let's make it $300, and I'll put it in the truck for you right now."

The guy started crying; he was so amazed that anybody would do that for him. He had arrived expecting to spend money he could barely afford, and instead he got a deal— and he didn't have to lift a finger!

D Is for Deliver Excellence

When my client told me that story, I was so proud just to know him. He's a person who truly delivers excellence.

Just think: in a matter of minutes, Andrew built a connection with this guy. He understood the transaction, and his strategy was to ensure that the chair went to the right home. It wasn't about making money. He led and inspired by going above and beyond. And that's what delivering excellence is all about.

Remember centrifugal looping? You can fully deliver excellence only after you have gone through the entire BUILD framework again. You have built relationships, you understand the business, you are implementing strategies, and you lead and inspire. And all of that takes you to a higher level, so you can be ready to truly deliver excellence.

Excellence is about what I call "the value of the vibe," or how your customer feels experientially. When you understand what your clients experience, you can have that heartfelt connection with them. At the end of the day, delivering excellence also includes tracking metrics, communicating well, and having good results. But within The BUILD Framework®, delivering excellence occurs when all of the BUILD elements come together in the heart.

When your heart is open and you are connected, you can deliver excellence on every level by ensuring that you feel it, inspecting what you expect, remembering the value of the vibe, and knowing that excellence is perpetual.

Feel It

The success attributes for delivering excellence, which we've been building up to throughout this entire book, are being open and connected. The previous success attributes lead you to deliver excellence—with patience and relating, nurturing and learning, discernment and will, and recognition and giving. All of those virtues ultimately come together in an open heart, allowing you to make stronger connections.

The emotional contractions are easy for this one: they are the exact opposites of the success attributes—being closed and disconnected. When we are closed off, we are back there in Struggleville, where people are disconnected from their feelings and have a really nice view of the Lake of Denial nearby. That's where you can see all those boats trying to paddle in different directions—until they capsize and the people inside them start to sink.

When you are not living in excellence, your heart and mind are closed, and so are your connections with your clients, your team, and your life.

You can deliver excellence only by understanding how to be open and connected. This is something you can't think your way through. You have to feel it.

Inspect What You Expect

Once you start experiencing life with an open heart, how can you deliver excellence in every arena? First, you want to measure what is important.

One thing you will always hear in the corporate world is to "know your metrics." But you deliver excellence when you don't just *know* your metrics—you also *understand* them. This goes back to understanding the business. You need to understand which metrics are important to deliver excellence.

Metrics drive behavior. And if you're tracking the wrong metrics, you're going to get the wrong behavior. You need to measure what matters.

When I worked at HP, counterfeiting was a huge problem. People could make a lot of money counterfeiting HP products, because they would build the products cheaply but sell them for the same price. For some organized criminal groups, it was much easier—and less risky—to make money by counterfeiting products than it was to sell cocaine and other drugs.

Even more than the lost revenue, counterfeiting damages the brand. Customers who get a printer that doesn't work think that HP isn't delivering excellence. So we had a whole anti-counterfeiting division that worked with law enforcement to run investigations.

One of the metrics the division tracked was the number of arrests of counterfeiters. But what behavior does tracking that metric drive? Making more arrests. Arrests were all well and good, of course, but we didn't want to catch only the twenty guys who were selling fake printers at some local shop. We wanted to track the shipping containers full of counterfeit products and find out who was actually doing the counterfeiting.

We changed that key metric to tracking not just arrests, but seizure values. How many dollars' worth of counterfeited products could we seize from these counterfeiters? Sometimes we had to wait for the right opportunity. Previously, we would have made quick arrests and brought in a couple hundred thousand dollars of merchandise. But now we were consistently confiscating multimillion-dollar shipments.

Adjusting that one key metric helped us reach our bigger goal of shutting down major criminal operations. And delivering that excellence was built upon every step of The BUILD Framework®. We built relationships with law enforcement. We understood the business more clearly and, as a result, adjusted which metrics we tracked. By implementing strategies that made sense for seizures instead of just arrests, we led and inspired our team to hit the goal, and, ultimately, we did.

You'll want to track metrics that make sense in your business. That means you inspect what you expect—metrics that motivate the behaviors you want to see. If you measure only how many phone calls somebody makes, making calls is the behavior that will be motivated. And if you have clients who take too long, asking difficult questions that will take a lot of time to address, what are they going to hear? The click of the dial tone as somebody hangs up and moves on to the next call.

Instead, try to have metrics in place that motivate your team to deliver excellence. If you expect something from your team, inspect it. If you don't measure it, how do you know if it improves?

And if you don't understand why you are tracking something, question it. You don't want to capture metrics just because you can. And the metrics you do capture should not be just about numbers and statistics. True understanding goes deeper, to the human element of behavior.

Understand the *why* behind all of the metrics, make sure they help you implement the *right* strategies, and ensure that every metric drives your team and your business to deliver excellence.

The Value of the Vibe

Another important concept for both you and your team to understand is that *how* you do something is oftentimes much more important than *what* you do.

Let's imagine it's your team's job to move a box from one room to another. If your team members move the box, but they are rude and belligerent and make other people angry, does the box get moved? Sure. And that's what the team is paid to do. But if your team members move the box and, in the process, they are happy and engaged and make other people laugh and enjoy life, that's delivering excellence.

It's not just about whether or not the box gets moved. It's about how it feels to you, your team, and your company. How does it feel to your customer? Again, it's about the value of the vibe.

What is the customer experience at your company? Have you walked through it? If you send out surveys, have you taken them? Have you even read them? Have you gone to your website and clicked through everything the way your clients would? Doing so allows you to discern what your customers go through. You need to ensure your customers' experience passes your value-of-the-vibe test.

Beyond that, you can also see how you and your team affect that experience. The way you act in your interactions shows whether you are putting more emphasis on *what* tasks you are doing versus *how* you do them. If your clients leave happy and smiling after every interaction with your team, you are certainly on your way to delivering excellence—and you may already be there. But smiles are just part of the goal. Strive to connect with the heart, and you will be able to go even deeper.

When you examine your processes from the perspective of your clients, it builds a deeper connection to them. And this is something your team can—and should—do as well. When you all have heart-centered connections, you are delivering excellence together.

Excellence Is Perpetual

Delivering excellence is not something that you do once and stop. Excellence is perpetual. That means you have to be in it for the long game.

Excellence also means not cutting corners.

If you and your employee agree that 25 percent of his or her time is to be spent building relationships, you can easily track that. If one week goes by and you realize no time was spent building relationships, that's only one week. But if two or three weeks go by, this is a problem, and you need to make midcourse corrections. In two weeks, you can remind your employee, "Hey, you need to spend some time actually building relationships."

And it's not just about how much time every employee spends on each letter in BUILD. It is as important—oftentimes more so—to ask what is being accomplished in each area. It's also about the deliverables. Remember, delivering excellence doesn't stop.

I consulted with one company that scheduled two-and-a-half-hour calls each week to review every metric from the previous week. That takes forever! And, of course, no one was listening on those calls. You could hear typing in the background. No one has that much time to spend each week looking backward instead of moving forward. Every time someone asked a question, I'd hear, "I'm sorry, could you repeat that?"

We went from that scenario to BUILD. We took fifteen minutes each week, not to go over how much time people spent, but to review the key accomplishments that were made. Employees would quickly report, "Here's the one thing I did last week that I'm proud of in building relationships." Then, "Here's how we moved forward in understanding the business." And so on.

Everyone listened and got excited—because they *got* it. They were all speaking the same language. They asked questions, which means they were engaged. And they were all clear on how to deliver excellence.

Excellence is perpetual—but your meetings don't have to be.

Action Benefit Challenge

The ABC for delivering excellence is to pick one metric and apply to it the same steps you have in the previous ABCs: identify it, verify it, solidify it, and engage. What is it? Why is it important? How am I going to do this? And then go do it!

What metric might you choose? How about putting The BUILD Framework® in place across your team? *Identify, check.*

Why is that important? Well, if I have to answer that at this point, you should probably stop reading here. Start over, read the entire book again, and then continue on. I'll wait.

Welcome back! Okay, now you know why it's important: so you can have success and growth in your life, personally and professionally. And so your team can have that as well. *Verify, check.*

How are you going to do this? Figure out how you want to communicate this new methodology, and write out your plan. Put it on your calendar. *Solidify, check.*

Now go do it. What does that mean? Put The BUILD Framework® in place. Explain it to your team. Have them report daily, weekly, or monthly—whatever makes sense for you. Try it on, and, as a leader, live it yourself. Make it yours. *Engage, check!*

When you and your team are living The BUILD Framework®, you will be connected. You will understand how to raise every interaction to the next level—and that is what delivering excellence is all about.

May I Take Your Order?

My wife and I went out to dinner at a beautiful restaurant while she was pregnant with our son. The food was delicious, the ambience was perfect, and the conversation was sparkling. The service, however, left something to be desired.

We had both selected vegan meals from the menu. (I promise this is not becoming a book about veganism!) When it came time for dessert, we asked the server about vegan options. She looked at us and then disappeared for a long time.

She finally returned. "The chef and I had to use Google to figure out what exactly vegan is. The vegan dessert is sorbet."

"What flavors do you have?" I asked.

She disappeared again. This time, she came back—only slightly faster—and recited, "We have strawberry, raspberry, and mango."

We decided to share the mango, so I asked for one scoop.

"I have to give you three scoops," the server said. "You can have three scoops of mango, or you can have one of each flavor."

"We want just the one scoop," I said. "We're happy to pay for all three, but we want you to bring us only one." We weren't really that hungry and did not want to waste two scoops that we knew we were not going to eat.

And she said, "I can't do that."

I looked around for cameras because it felt like I was on one of those TV comedy shows that does practical jokes on unsuspecting customers.

At this point, it had been more than half an hour from when we first asked about vegan desserts. I would have gladly paid for six scoops, just to have them bring us one! But rather than fighting it and arguing with a clearly confused server, I just asked for the check—and we had a good laugh.

That server didn't deliver dessert—or excellence!

You have come to the end of The BUILD Framework®— but beyond this ladder is another step. Turn the page to see how to BUILD even more success in your life by taking it to the next level.

Chapter 7

The Next Level

When leaving the nest,
look ahead and take flight.
For in looking back,
you turn day into night.

Divine Love

As I told you at the beginning of this book, I am on my fourth marriage. Once I applied BUILD to my personal relationships, not just my business ventures—and learned to connect with the heart—I was able to experience true growth and lasting success in all areas of my life. I was able to obtain balance.

I always had a strategy to implement in my relationships, and that included different ways to manifest my mate. One main practice was to write down all the things I wanted in that person—specific details such as what she looked like and how she acted. The next step was to say, "And please, Universe, make her even better." Sometimes, you just have to *think* it.

My first wife had been my high school sweetheart. That marriage was very short; it lasted only a couple of years. She left because she needed to "discover herself."

One night, as I was driving a long distance to Mystic Lake Casino, I thought very specifically about what I was looking for in a second mate. I imagined she'd be younger than I was and gorgeous, with long dark hair. She'd be wearing white jeans, a black leotard, and a white vest with fringe on it. And if the relationship were to work out, she'd have to live close to me.

About an hour into the evening, I walked across the room to the blackjack area, and there she was: sitting at a blackjack table and wearing that *exact* outfit! I sat down next to her and tried to impress her by betting large sums of money. That part didn't work (I lost a ton), but she did become my second wife. And—get this—she had lived only two blocks away from my house all along!

Again, it didn't work out. Once again, I had found someone who ultimately decided to leave me in order to more fully discover herself.

Again, I thought about what I wanted in a new mate. I realized that my past wish lists were superficial, and I was determined that this one would be different. I wrote down the following: "I want to meet a professional who has a successful career and knows herself, has her own money, and has been in a relationship before." In fact, I included that she'd have been married before—after all, I was going on my third—and understood the business of marriage: a "perfect partner," I wrote. I made it very clear that location did not matter this time.

That's what I requested, so that is what I got. Every single item! She had just attended a "perfect partner" workshop. And, get this: she lived in Australia!

But because I basically wrote up a business proposal, our marriage ended like many business arrangements when one partner demands out—in dissolution. And I was thrice divorced.

At that point, you might think I'd give up. But not me! I did, however, decide not to be too specific. I learned my lesson—be careful what you ask for!—and I put only two words out into the Universe: divine love.

Eventually, I met Marliesa. One night, we went out to dinner at Blue Ginger, a restaurant on Darling Street near my house in Australia. As we waited for our food, we started talking about the past. And I said, "All I've put out there now is just 'divine love.'"

Before I could blink, she rolled up her sleeve to show me a tattoo on her wrist, one she'd gotten years before. And it was an Arabic symbol meaning "divine love."

That was the moment it hit me in the heart: this is the *one*. And she and I never looked back as we stepped into divine love together.

BUILD a Houseboat

Even after my success incorporating The BUILD Framework® in the corporate environment, I still had to ask myself, "What am I doing in my personal life?"

And once I said, "Enough is enough," it struck me: the BUILD boat isn't just for work. It's a houseboat, too.

Because the boat works. Before, I would get out of the boat every day, I would go home, and then I would sink into the Lake of Denial. But now that I know BUILD can be a houseboat, too, it's present in every part of my life.

I first had to build relationships with myself, my wife, and my family. I had to take care of myself—my health and my personal time—as well as look after others. I had to understand the business of marriage and of the relationships that are important to me. Then I could implement strategies. And let me tell you now: I never miss a date night! As for my children, I ask myself, "How can I lead and inspire them? How can Daddy be the hero? And how am I delivering excellence in those relationships?"

As soon as I did that, things worked out.

You can do the same. BUILD is not just about your business. Don't forget about the value of the vibe at home. If you are reading this book and planning to apply BUILD to your work environment and not your home life, stop right now. Ask yourself what you are doing.

Yes, this is an amazing framework for your business. But it's even *more* amazing and brilliant for your home and your life. How do you build relationships at home—and with yourself? How do you understand the business of your *life*? What strategies do you implement at home? How do you lead and inspire there? What does delivering excellence mean to you? How does excellence feel at home?

By delivering excellence at the level that helps you become successful, your family, your community—your entire world—becomes more successful as well.

Your life and your excellence are not about metrics. It's not about getting millions of dollars. It's about who you are and how you experience this very moment. Because this moment *is* your life!

Are you ensuring balance across all these areas of BUILD so you don't get lost in just one? This is probably the most important point of all. When you don't have balance, you will never find true success. And when you do have balance in life, you have the ability to—as my company's motto will remind you—turn stress, struggle, and strife into health, happiness, and harmony in *all* areas of your life.

Get Schooled

The other day, I talked to a student group about the BUILD concept.

A kid who had just turned sixteen came up to me and said, "That's so cool! Hey, JP, can you please give all of our teachers this book?"

I asked him why.

And he told me: "If my teachers understood they had to first build relationships with us, it would change the whole school. But they don't. They're up there trying to deliver excellence or trying to lead, but they're not going to. They don't have a relationship with anyone."

I was blown away. He was right. This doesn't apply just to my life or to your business. It applies *everywhere*.

He wasn't done yet, though. He had really thought this through. "If our teachers build a good relationship with the students," he continued, "that relationship could help us understand the business of learning. The teachers could figure out the right strategies to implement to help us learn. Then if they lead and inspire us—I mean, that's what teachers are supposed to do—they would be delivering excellence!"

I couldn't do much more than smile and say, "Yeah, mate. Can I write that down? That's pretty cool!"

That day, in that schoolyard, I was the one who got schooled on my own framework.

Your Success Is My Success

You know everything you need to know to have success in your life. And now you have a framework to organize all of that knowledge so you can access it when you need it. At this point, it's no longer just about making things happen. It's about making things stick.

That's what I am encouraging and challenging you to do now: make it stick.

And if you need help with that, I am here for you. Reach out at any time, and I will work directly with you to find and implement the tools and techniques to fill your BUILD file cabinet. You don't have to go it alone. It is my joy to have the opportunity to work with people who have a vision, who have a dream, but who haven't quite figured out how to get it to this next level. I would love to help you do more while increasing the overall balance in your life.

The BUILD Framework® allows you to learn those techniques, access them when you need to, and apply them to your life. I can work with you individually or with your team or corporation to implement this framework for greater personal development, deeper connections, and more success.

If you've already started applying The BUILD Framework®, I'd love to hear your success stories, too. You can reach me at www.TheBuildFramework.com, where you can also find additional resources to support your journey of understanding and application.

Just know that every single person who uses The BUILD Framework® makes it his or her own. And now you can make it yours.

A New Beginning

Congratulations! You've reached the end. I want to applaud you for your effort.

And I want to send you back on your journey. Because this end is truly a new beginning.

Whether this is your first time reading this book, or if you've been here several times before, you know that you have so many paths ahead of you. The ones you choose are essentially limitless!

You have an amazing life. And with your center of gravity shifted from your head to your heart, you will be able to appreciate it in a way you may not have had the opportunity to before. Feel it.

Everything is aligned in this moment. Feel your heart expand. Experience your new baseline.

And get ready for your life to grow and become even more amazing!

KEEP BUILDING!

Congratulations! You've come this far, and now you are inspired to take action to see how The BUILD Framework® can positively influence your life and provide lasting transformation.

The good news is that you do not have to do this in a vacuum. You are not alone. There is a wealth of information and support waiting for you within a community of people who are, like you, actively engaged in using BUILD to improve themselves and those around them.

The BUILD Framework® website is a place where you can:

- Access resources and tools to support your journey of understanding and application, including specific worksheets and downloads

- Discover even more valuable information to help you live your life to the fullest, and come to understand more fully how to take your success to the next level

- Meet a heart-based tribe that is connected through our mutual desire to significantly increase the momentum in your life propelling you toward your dreams and desires

Don't stop now!

Are you ready to BUILD even more success into your personal and professional life? Put these changes you have learned into action.

Continue the momentum by visiting:

www.TheBUILDFramework.com

ABOUT THE AUTHOR

John Peitzman, or JP, is a lifelong expert in the art of high performance. From his time as a young performing artist to his executive career spanning the globe, JP has embraced and cultivated his entrepreneurial spirit throughout his life.

One of only a couple hundred elite High Performance Institute–certified coaches worldwide, JP left the corporate world in 2015 and founded *In Balance with Life* with his wife, Marliesa. *He is passionate about helping business owners, entrepreneurs, and corporate teams get to the next level by teaching them the most advanced high-performance techniques available in the world, so that they can turn stress, struggle, and strife into health, happiness, and harmony . . . and obtain true balance in their lives.*

JP is also a senior practitioner of AcuEnergetics® (a comprehensive energetic healing modality), a meditation teacher, a highly sought-after speaker and life coach, as well as a fifth-degree black belt martial arts head instructor. He leverages his broad background to show clients how to effectively integrate ancient healing techniques, proven business methodologies, and high-performance habits into their personal lives to help increase awareness, health, joy, and success.

JP is the founder of The AWESOME Life Club and currently lives in Australia with his wife, Marliesa, and two children, Myah and Jacob. You can learn more about his journey by listening to his reading of an original poem, "The Wake of Ambition," at:

www.TheWakeOfAmbition.com